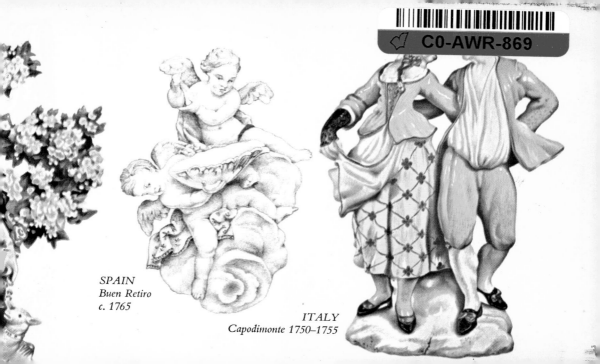

SPAIN
Buen Retiro
c. 1765

ITALY
Capodimonte 1750–1755

ABOUT THE COVER: *The Passionate Suitor* by Franz Anton Bustelli; circa 1760.

ACKNOWLEDGMENTS: 2 (center and right) *Victoria and Albert Museum, London*; 3 (left) *Victoria and Albert Museum*, (right) *Fitzwilliam Museum, Cambridge, England*; 6 Reproduced with the permission of Mr. and Mrs. George P. Bissell, Jr.; 8 (left) *Cooper Union Museum, New York*; 10 (left) *Cooper Union Museum*; 14 *The Metropolitan Museum of Art*; 16 *Musée Jacquemart André*; 17 (left) *Victoria and Albert Museum*, (right) *British Museum*; 18 (left) *National Museum of Wales*, (right) *Cooper Union Museum*; 21 (left) *The Metropolitan Museum of Art, Gift of the Estate of James Hazen Hyde, 1959*; 24 (left) *Hon. Irwin Untermyer*, (right) *Bayerisches Nationalmuseum, München*; 25 (top right and right) *Cooper Union Museum*; 27 *New York Public Library, Arents Collection*; 28 (left) *Victoria and Albert Museum*, (right) *Osterreichisches Museum für Angewandte Kunst, Vienna*; 29, 30 *Cooper Union Museum*; 33 (left) *The Antique Porcelain Company, New York*, (right) *Wallace Collection, London*; 34 *Propyläen Verlag, Berlin*; 35 *Museo di Capodimonte, Napoli*; 37 (left) *Hon. Irwin Untermyer*, (right) *The Shand-Kydd Collection, Bedfordshire, England*; 39 (left) *Hon. Irwin Untermyer*, (right) *Museo Duca di Martina, Napoli*; 40 *Georg Jensen, New York*; 41 *Cooper Union Museum*; 43 (left) *The Metropolitan Museum of Art, Collection of Helena Woolworth McCann*, (right) *The Philadelphia Museum of Art*; 46 (left) *Bayerisches Nationalmuseum*, (right) *Victoria and Albert Museum*; 47 (left and right) *Bayerisches Nationalmuseum*, (center) *Museum für Kunst und Gewerbe, Hamburg*.

THE STORY OF PORCELAIN

BY HEDY BACKLIN-LANDMAN

**CURATOR OF DECORATIVE ARTS
THE COOPER UNION MUSEUM**

AND EDNA SHAPIRO

ILLUSTRATED BY HARRY McNAUGHT

THE ODYSSEY PRESS · NEW YORK

It was a rage, a craze, a madness, this mania for collecting china that swept Europe in the 18th century. Caught up in it were kings and princes, chemists and alchemists, potters and painters and sea captains and merchants. Tea and silks and sailing ships played a part in it, but the real cause was the ware that came from China—ceramic vessels of a substance called porcelain. ■ The name was bestowed by Marco Polo, the Venetian traveler; the gleaming vessels he saw at the court of Kublai Khan reminded him of the sea shell called *porcella*.

French and American "Hongs" or trade offices at Canton, China, in the early 19th century, painted by an unknown Chinese artist. Foreigners were allowed to stay here during the trading season to transact business.

■ Europe had no ware so hard, so durable, so beautiful—white in body, smooth to the touch, translucent where thin, and resonant, chiming like a bell when struck. Europe had pottery, of course. Majolica and faience—earthenware with an opaque tin glaze—could be beautiful, too, especially when decorated with scenes and figures by artists who painted in the grand style of the Renaissance. But the Chinese had some secret way of transforming clay into a substance of such delicacy that Europe's wares seemed crude, coarse, almost primitive. ■ No wonder, then, that Europe's monarchs sought porcelain as a precious rarity, to be cherished like jewels or finely wrought silver and gold. As early as 1447, the Sultan of Egypt presented King Charles VII of France with several pieces

Blue and white Chinese porcelain jar with lotus, pine and plum tree design painted underneath the glaze. Yüan dynasty (1280–1368)

of porcelain. The Medici treasured porcelain along with their antiquities of Greece and Rome. Queen Elizabeth of England prized "a poringer of white porselyn and a cup of green porselyn." ■ There is evidence that the Chinese knew the technique of making porcelain as

The pencil drawings at left show a covered urn from the T'ang dynasty (618–906) and a bottle with incised pattern, of celadon ware, from the Sung dynasty (960–1279). The precursors of Chinese porcelain, they have neither the whiteness nor the translucency of true porcelain.

early as 700, in the T'ang dynasty (618-906). ■ The secret of true, or hard-paste, porcelain lay in the materials and the firing. One of the materials was kaolin, a white china clay which is an aluminum silicate; the other was a feldspathic rock ground into a powder, known as *pai-tun-tzu* in China and petuntse in the West. Kaolin does not fuse even at extremely high temperatures; petuntse, a silicate of potassium and aluminum, fuses at about 1,450 degrees Centigrade. ■ The glaze, the thin, hard, glass-

9

like outer skin of porcelain, also consisted of petuntse. It was applied to the body of the object as a fluid, and then fired. ■ The body of a porcelain piece was shaped, like any pottery, on a potter's wheel or by a mold. It could be decorated with colors painted on before the glaze was applied, or painted on afterward and refired. ■ The first great period of Chinese porcelain came in the Sung dynasty (960-1279). Outstanding was the ware later called celadon, which had a green glaze and decorations incised in the body before glazing. The Chinese valued it highly because it resembled jade. ■

Chinese overglaze colors on the platter and the vase, called "famille rose" and "famille verte," were favored by 18th-century European collectors over earlier types such as those on the small bowl. Rust red, blue and a fresh green were the dominant colors on Japanese porcelain decorated in the style of Kakiemon in the 17th century, as shown in detail at right.

Workrooms in a porcelain factory, engraved about 1770 by Nicolas de la Ransonette. At left, vases are being decorated; in the background, painted objects are being fired in the muffle or enamel kiln; at right, pigments are being prepared.

These are all steps in the making of fired and glazed pieces. In a separate workroom at the far right, two workmen called "repairers" assemble the freshly molded parts of figurines. The original figurine, modeled by the master modeler, is cut

into pieces and separate molds are made from the head, arms, legs, and other sections. The castings taken from these molds are then reassembled with liquid clay, called slip, while still wet. In this way, a number of figurines could be produced.

The second great period was the Ming dynasty (1368-1644), when Ching-techen, near the city of Nanking, became the center of porcelain manufacture. Under the patronage of the emperors and the supervision of state officials, Ching-techen would flourish for centuries to come. During the Ming dynasty were produced the bowls of "eggshell" porcelain, so thin that the Chinese called them *t'o t'ai*—bodiless. Even more important, however, were the introduction of painted decoration in various colors, and the development of blue-and-white ware, with decorations painted in underglaze blue. During the reigns of the Ch'ing emperors, K'ang Hsi (1662-1722), Yung Cheng (1723-1735), and Ch'ien Lung (1736-1795), the artistry and technical mastery of the craftsmen were at their height, and the variety and quantity of the wares turned out at Ching-techen were stagger-

13

ing. In the early 1700's, more than a million people lived there and 3000 kilns were in operation, and the fires of the furnaces lit up the sky. ■ This period saw the development of polychrome wares with one dominant color, known in Europe as *famille verte* (green), *famille jaune* (yellow), *famille noire* (black), and *famille rose* (pink). During this period the Chinese also produced for export a ware often called "Oriental Lowestoft," painted to order with armorial insignia or other typically Western decorations. The name was an error perpetrated by the Victorian scholar William Chaffers, who believed the ware was made in the English village of Lowestoft. The error was discovered but the name remained, especially in America. ■ A more accurate name is "China-trade porcelain," for by the 18th century China was doing a brisk export business with the West. First to reach China were the

Drug jar from Faenza, Italy (LEFT) and platter from Valencia, Spain (UPPER RIGHT) are fifteenth-century attempts to imitate the colorful appearance of Oriental porcelain. The reddish-buff clay was covered with an opaque white glaze and then painted, a method invented in the Near East and brought to Spain by the Arabs.

Seventeenth-century Dutch jar from Delft with opaque white glaze over buff clay. The blue underglaze painting was inspired by Chinese porcelain imported to Holland.

Portuguese; they were followed by the Dutch, the English, and a number of others, including the French, the Swedes, the Danes, and, finally, the Americans. They came for silks and tea, but the ships' masters found that crates of neatly packed porcelain made excellent ballast and could be sold at home.
■ It was the West's enthusiasm for tea and the other newly introduced beverages, coffee and chocolate, that set off the demand for porcelain. Nowhere was there such a thirst for tea as in England, where ale had long been the customary breakfast drink and even children were given their "small beer." Suddenly pewter and silver mugs, good enough for beer, were out of fashion; they seemed too gross for the exotic, fragrant tea, and, besides, they conducted heat. The English clamored for delicate tea cups of "Chinaware"—and the great Chinamania was on. Soon they also clamored for tea pots, saucers, dishes, and plates as well; many ordered tea and dinner services decorated to their fancy, even though they had

Spouted vessel of so-called Medici porcelain, painted with underglaze blue. Kaolinic earth from the region of Vicenza was used by the Florentines in a successful attempt to achieve a fine, white, translucent ceramic body.

Johann Friedrich Böttger (1682–1719), discoverer of the composition of European porcelain. The medallion and the teapot are of red stoneware, Böttger's first discovery in collaboration with chemist-physicist Ehrenfried Walter von Tschirnhausen, in 1708.

Covered vase of white Böttger porcelain, with relief decoration. Meissen, 1715–1720.

Meissen teapot with chinoiserie decoration by Johann Gregor Herold, about 1724. Coffee pot with "German flowers" (Deutsche Blumen), mid-18th century.

Candy dish in the shape of a shell held by a triton is part of a 1500-piece table service with sea motifs, called the Swan service. It was modeled in Meissen by master modeler Johann Joachim Kändler for Count Brühl, director of the factory, between 1737 and 1741.

to wait two years for delivery. ■ The craze for porcelain rapidly spread over Europe and to America. Monarchs and nobles competed more fiercely than ever for rarities and fine pieces. For a time their taste ran to the blue-and-white wares of the late Ming and K'ang Hsi periods; so esteemed were these wares that the Dutch copied their patterns in the white glazed earthenware called Delft, after the town where it was made in large quantities. ■ Kings and princes also collected porcelain from Japan, which had learned the secret from China in the 16th century. Most prized were the Kakiemon wares with delicate enameling, and the Imari wares decorated in brocade patterns. ■ Of all the royal collectors, the most avid was Augustus the Strong, Elector of Saxony and King of Poland. He once gave the king of Prussia a regiment of dragoons in exchange for 48 vases he coveted. He spent thousands of thalers on his collection, and a Saxon nobleman said that China was "the bleeding bowl of Saxony." ■ The nobleman was Ehrenfried Walter von Tschirnhausen; he was a chemist as well, and about 1694 he began searching for the secret of porcelain. In 1704 he acquired Johann Friedrich Böttger as his assistant. ■ Böttger was an alchemist whom Augustus had brought to Dresden to turn base metal into gold. Unable to produce gold, Böttger tried to escape, only to be hauled back and ordered to make gold with Tschirnhausen. ■ The two failed, of course, and Böttger was thrown into prison. But Tschirnhausen, who had already come close to discovering the secret of porcelain, asked that Böttger be released to help him. ■ Over the door of his laboratory, Böttger later wrote: *God our Creator has made a potter out of a goldmaker.* He collaborated diligently with Tschirnhausen, and in 1708 the two men produced an extremely hard red stoneware that could be cut on a lapidary's wheel like a gem stone. Tschirnhausen died that same year, and the following year Böttger announced that he could make "good white porcelain together with the finest glaze and appropriate painting in such perfection as to equal if not surpass the East Indian." ■ Augustus was quick to take advantage of this tremendous achievement; in 1710 he founded the Royal Saxon Porcelain Manufacture at Dresden and put Böttger in charge. A few months later the factory was moved to nearby Meissen. At first things did not go well. Böttger was no administrator, and his years under Augustus' thumb had driven him to drink. When he died in 1719, Augustus appointed a commission to supervise the factory, which then began to thrive. ■ The basic process of making porcelain was now established. First the raw materials—quartz, kaolin and feldspar—were ground and mixed with water. Out of this soft mass, cups and circular dishes were made on the potter's wheel; other shapes were pressed in plaster molds. Figurines were modeled. Some were used as originals, while others were cut up into parts from which molds were made, so that the figure

Meissen figurine by Kändler, about 1746, after the allegoric drawing of Africa by G. B. Götz. Drawings and engravings often served as inspiration for porcelain pieces. Well-known artists such as François Boucher and Etienne Maurice Falconet provided the factories with original sketches for decorations and models for figurines.

The Passionate Suitor, *by Franz Anton
Bustelli, Nymphenburg, c. 1760. The ardor
of the young man whom Amor tries to restrain
and the frightened recoil of the object of his
passion are delightfully depicted in Bustelli's
typically vivacious manner.*

could be reproduced in quantity. ■ A first firing in the kiln at 1500-1800° F, called bisque firing, made the ware hard enough to be handled further. Underglaze decoration in cobalt blue or other metallic oxides was then painted on, and the piece dipped into the liquid glaze. Consisting largely of the same feldspathic component as the porcelain itself, the glaze was completely fused with the body in the second firing at 2500-2650° F. Enamel colors that could not withstand the high temperature were then painted on top of the glaze and refired in a "muffle" kiln at 1200-1450° F, often in a succession of firings to fix the various colors properly. Gilding was the last step, fired at even lower temperatures and then burnished. ■ Augustus bought the Dutch Palace at Dresden-Neustadt and converted it into what he called the Japanese Palace—a vast showcase for his collection of Oriental and Meissen wares. Although never completed, the Japanese Palace contained more than 35,000 pieces of porcelain, including many large vases and figures of animals. Other monarchs and princes also displayed their collections in "porcelain rooms" in their palaces. ■ When Augustus died in 1733, the factory passed into the hands of his son, Augustus III. The great years of Meissen's glory had already begun, and they would continue until 1756. Johann Gregor Herold had become head of the painting shop in 1720, and in 1733 the sculptor Johann Joachim Kändler, one of the greatest artists in the field of porcelain, became the master modeler. Herold developed new colors and decorative elements, while Kändler modeled the typical Dresden figures, works of wonderful charm, wit, and spirit. ■ Kändler turned out more than 1,000 figurines—animals, birds, chinoiseries, folk figures, and commedia del' arte and court figurines, often

Fantastic and whimsical objects have always had a strong appeal to both makers and collectors of porcelain. LEFT TO RIGHT: Meissen teapot, Nymphenburg cane handle, Bow candelabrum, Meissen knife handle, Frankenthal Pierrot scent bottle, Chinese wigstand made for the European market.

Factory marks were usually incised in the bottom of the piece, or painted on in colors. They varied considerably over the years and were often copied by other makers.

Meissen   *Vienna*   *Frankenthal*   *Nymphenburg*   *Chantilly*

with a touch of satire. He also modeled many vessels, including the elaborate Swan service. ■ Over the years, Meissen produced a vast quantity and variety of pieces. Painted decorations on services included the *Deutsche Blumen,* naturalistic German flowers, which were widely imitated by other makers. ■ Although the factory directors frowned on it, they could not stop the practice of *Hausmalerei,* "home painting." The *Hausmaler* procured white porcelain pieces and painted them at home or in a small shop, often in a personal style and with great skill. ■ In 1756, Saxony fell to Frederick the Great of Prussia, who carried off the stock of the Meissen factory and commanded it to make a num-

ber of dinner services to his order. The factory continued in operation, but its greatest period had come to an end. ■ The directors of Meissen had done everything in their power to guard their secret, but a disgruntled employee carried it to Vienna, where Europe's second hard-paste factory was established in 1719. The secret then passed through a number of hands until it was purchased by a financier, who, with the aid of two more disgruntled Meissen employees, opened a factory in Berlin in 1761. Frederick bought it two years later, and was determined to make it pay. ■ The rulers of Germany's many small states, jealous of the gold and glory of Meissen, managed to get the secret one way

Berlin *Sèvres* *Chelsea* *Copenhagen* *Naples*

or another and set up their own porcelain factories. The most notable was at Nymphenburg, under the patronage of Max Joseph III, Elector of Bavaria. His wife was a daughter of Augustus III, who had inherited the Meissen factory. Nymphenburg had a famous master modeler in Franz Anton Bustelli (1723-63), considered by some authorities at least as great as Kändler. He produced figurines of tremendous verve and

The new fashion of tea and coffee drinking stimulated the growth of the European porcelain industry. Tea was expensive and the early pots as well as the handleless cups were small; drinking from the saucer was permissible. Jars and vases were collected as ornaments for wall shelves, mantel shelves, or specially built cabinets.

vitality, especially his 16 characters of the "Italian Comedy." ■ But not everyone could find runaway employees of Meissen, and for centuries potters had been desperately trying to discover the secret of porcelain for themselves. Out of their efforts came soft-paste porcelain, made of white clay, ground glass and various other ingredients. Although soft-paste porcelain had a beauty and delicacy of its own, it was not true porcelain. Furthermore, it was extremely difficult and costly to produce. Another attempt to imitate porcelain was the milk glass (often painted with blue), made in Venice from the 16th century on. ■ Soft-paste porcelain was

Tankard with silver mounts, c. 1735, and coffee pot, 1720, from du Paquier's factory in Vienna, the second in Europe to make true porcelain. Leopard handle and bearded mask on coffee pot are characteristic of baroque style of early Vienna ware. Flowers on tankard are early version of "German flowers," still somewhat under Oriental influence.

Detail of centerpiece with figures representing Asia, Europe and America (Africa is on the other side), Ludwigsburg, c. 1765. Table decorations often consisted of dozens of individual figurines, as in the set from Berlin given by Frederick the Great to Catherine of Russia in 1770.

produced in Italy as early as 1575, when Francesco Maria de' Medici, Grand Duke of Tuscany, set up a factory in the Boboli Gardens. The magnificent pieces turned out here became known as Medici porcelain. ■ At Doccia, near Florence, in a factory founded by the Marchese Carlo Ginori in 1735, a porcelain closer to hard-paste was produced, called *masso bastardo*. ■ Fine soft-paste was made at the Capodimonte factory, near Naples, established in 1743 by King Charles of the Two Sicilies. Much of his inspiration came from the quantities of Meissen ware that were part of his wife's dowry; she

Covered dish of soft paste from Chantilly, France, about 1735, the flowers inspired by Japanese porcelain in the collection of the Prince de Condé, founder of the factory. Attempts to make porcelain with the admixture of ground glass resulted in a multitude of formulas that varied considerably but produced a softer ware than true porcelain, hence the name "soft paste."

was another daughter of Augustus III. When Charles became king of Spain in 1759, he moved the porcelain factory to the palace of Buen Retiro, near Madrid; some hard-paste porcelain was also turned out here between 1804 and 1808. King Charles' son, Ferdinand IV, fell heir to the throne of the Two Sicilies as a boy. When he grew up his interest in porcelain was kindled and he founded a factory at Portici in 1771, but moved it to Naples two years later. Most of the porcelain produced here was in the neo-classical style, exemplified by the large "Herculaneum" service decorated with copies of wall-paintings found in the ruins of the ancient Roman town. This service was a gift to Charles III of Spain, while an "Etruscan" set was presented to George III of England. ■ In France, soft-paste porcelain had been made at Rouen since the late 17th century. Saint Cloud, Chantilly, Mennecy, and Vincennes followed. A

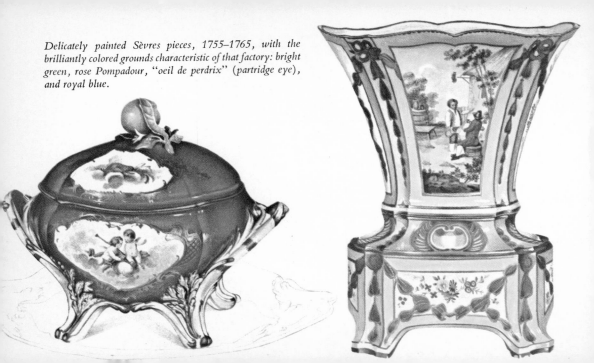

Delicately painted Sèvres pieces, 1755–1765, with the brilliantly colored grounds characteristic of that factory: bright green, rose Pompadour, "oeil de perdrix" (partridge eye), and royal blue.

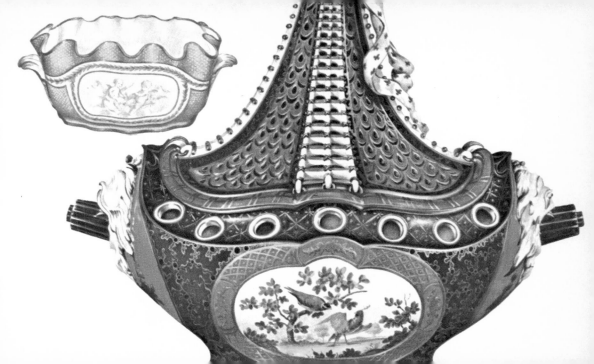

patron of Vincennes was still another daughter of Augustus III, Maria Josepha, who had married the Dauphin. But persons of even higher station were interested in this factory. King Louis XV's mistress, Madame de Pompadour, persuaded him to buy a fourth interest in the factory when it ran into financial difficulties. It was moved to Sèvres in 1756, and three years later Louis took it over entirely; it became the *Manufacture Royale de Porcelaine*. As such, it produced pieces of extravagant magnificence— and enormous expense. Louis used them in his royal palaces and, according to a contemporary account, "as presents for his relatives, his friends, his courtiers, and his ambassadors." The factory was seldom free of financial troubles. But Louis placed severe restrictions on other French porcelain manufacturers, and he and the Pompadour constantly urged members of the court to buy the royal wares. And every

New Year's Day, an eyewitness wrote, "they bring into the galleries at Versailles the newest and choicest pieces...which the King himself distributes among his great lords for their money; he fixes the prices himself and they are not cheap.... It is certain that some of the noble lords are not ashamed of taking a cup, or some little ornament, when they think they are not observed." ■ In 1769 Sèvres began to produce hard-paste porcelain. Louis XVI also took an active interest in Sèvres, as did Marie Antoinette. During the Revolution, the factory fell

Interior of the porcelain room made for Queen Maria Amalia by Giuseppe Gricc at the Capodimonte factory near Naples, 1757–1759. The porcelain collections at Charlottenburg, Pommersfelden, Schönbrunn and other royal and princely residences, were displayed on gilded and lacquered shelves and consoles, but this room and its copy at Aranjuez near Madrid were entirely covered with porcelain reliefs, as shown in detail at right.

on hard times, but in 1800 Napoleon had it reorganized. In 1876 it was made a national institution, with a subsidy and an advisory committee of potters, artists, and critics; it is still in operation today. ■ During its years of production, the Vincennes-Sèvres enterprise introduced new colors and a number of other innovations. Among them were the enormously popular porcelain flowers, sometimes on metal stems. Madame de Pompadour once surprised Louis with an indoor garden of such flowers, suitably scented. Other innovations were biscuit ware, an unglazed porcelain; and pâte-sur-pâte, painting in relief with semi-liquid white slip on a tinted ground. ■ By the end of the 18th century there were few countries in Europe that did not produce some porcelain, and an important center of porcelain manufacture rose at Copenhagen, Denmark. Here, in 1789, was begun the celebrated *Flora Danica* service. Despite evidence to the contrary, it is generally believed that this service was made as a gift from the Danish king to the Empress Catherine II of Russia. ■ China collecting was widespread in England, which imported great quantities of Oriental and European wares. Soft paste of varying composition was produced at Bow, Chelsea, and other factories. In an attempt to produce hard-paste porcelain, Edward Heylyn and Thomas Frye went so far as to import clay from the New World. "The material," said their patent application of 1744, "is an earth, the

Teapot from Longton Hall, about 1755, and perfume vase from Chelsea, 1765, show different influences in English porcelain. The tulip petals and stalks of the teapot are evidence of the 18th century's concern with nature, while the colorful butterfly is clearly of Oriental inspiration. Monochrome painting in reserve on plain ground, whether a figure scene or a landscape, is typical of a taste for pictorial representation that lasted well into the 19th century.

produce of the Cherokee nation in America, called by the natives *unaker.*" However, not until 1768 was hard paste successfully produced in England. ■ But England contributed something new and distinctive to porcelain—bone china, a kind of hard paste made with the addition of a substantial amount of bone ash. The formula was fully developed by Josiah Spode of Stoke-on-Trent, around 1800, and was soon adopted by most English factories. ■ Although Josiah Wedgwood (1730-1795) made no porcelain or bone china during his lifetime, he had a great influence on the production of porcelain. Not only did he introduce new forms, inspired chiefly by the pottery and sculpture of ancient Greece, but he also developed mass production methods and new kinds

Birds and animals were part of the realm of porcelain. Kändler impressed Augustus the Strong with his life-size swans, eagles and dogs, but too often they cracked during the firing and had to be discarded. Far more suitable to the material were the smaller versions of animals and birds that were made in such abundance and delightful variety at almost all factories, as individual figurines or as parts of domestic and hunting groups.

Quetzal and peacock by Kändler, Meissen; owl by Stefano Gricc, Capodimonte (RIGHT), and Chelsea daw (BELOW). Such figurines were as much an expression of the 18th century's delight in the spectacular colors of plumage as of its newly awakened interest in nature.

Dessert plate with daffodil from the Flora Danica service, Copenhagen. The openwork border was perforated by hand, as were the basket-shaped dessert dishes. Regular plates and serving pieces had "pearl" edge (BELOW).

of ceramic materials, the most notable being cream ware and jasper ware. ■ While many of the old factories such as Meissen, Berlin, Sèvres, Worcester, and Derby continued to flourish during the 19th century, others succumbed to competition. New ceramic industrial centers arose in Bavaria, in the French city of Limoges, and in the United States, in New Jersey and Ohio. In the second half of the century, the general revival of interest in handicrafts led many artists and amateurs to turn to porcelain painting. While such artists as Theodore Deck in France and M. L. Solon and Emile Lessore in England produced highly refined individual pieces, much of the output of the porcelain factories was heavily overdecorated or imitative of earlier styles. ■ In keeping with the more restrained taste of the mid-20th century, porcelain factories have now introduced simpler and better-designed wares. The design-

Cup with decoration in silver and gold, Berlin, about 1810. One of the few early factories to survive the changing tastes of the turn of the century, Berlin soon adapted the French Empire style to its production. The Sèvres factory excelled in impressive but somewhat overdecorated pieces in this style.

Each of the 1802 pieces in the Flora Danica service was painted with a different flower, sprig, or bud, copied from a botanical work of the same name which recorded the plants of Denmark and its possessions. The full set was never finished, but delivery—without payment—was made to the royal household at Amalienborg in 1803.

ing of both shapes and decoration is done either in the studios or the factories or by independent designers, such as the American Richard Latham, the Dane Bjørn Wiinblad, and the Finn Tapio Wirkkala. Their designs for various factories in their native lands, as well as for the internationally oriented Rosenthal factory in Germany, range from the severely simple to the whimsical. The vogue of porcelain figurines has subsided, and only a few pieces of quality are being produced in the contemporary style, while factories such as Nymphenburg continue to repeat their old models, usually without the painted decoration. ■ Porcelain throughout its long development has reflected many facets of our past. The influence of the Orient, the rise of world trade, new discoveries in science, advances in industrial processes—all played a part in its history. The craft of porcelain making reached its peak in that delightfully sophisticated era, the mid-18th century, and mirrors that age perhaps better than any other art form of the period. The playful figurines tell anecdotes of their time, the beautifully shaped and decorated vessels speak of the grace and elegance of court life, and the brightly colored birds and vigorously modeled animals reveal a joy in the beauty of nature. ■ Porcelain produced in other ages has its own kind of beauty, and historical associations add to the fascination it exerts. No wonder, then, that porcelain remains a delight to the eye and the touch. Fine pieces are preserved and exhibited in museums and studied by scholars, and collecting, while not the widespread mania of the 18th century, is still the passion of many connoisseurs. ■

Teapot with the arms of the United States; Chinese export porcelain made for the American market, 1795–1800. Vase by Tucker and Hemphill of Philadelphia, about 1835, with gilt bronze handles. This first production of hard porcelain in the United States was an attempt to compete with foreign imports. Despite its successful results in the composition of the material and the decoration, the factory closed after thirteen years.

CHRONOLOGY

8th century A.D. (T'ang dynasty, China): first porcellaneous ware. **851:** reports, by an Arab merchant, of Chinese vessels "translucent and as fine as glass." **960-1279** (Sung dynasty): celadon and white translucent "Ting" ware. **1271:** Marco Polo's journey from Venice to the court of Kublai Khan where he saw vessels resembling "porcella" shells. **1280-1368** (Yüan dynasty): first white porcelain with underglaze blue decoration. **1368-1643** (Ming dynasty): development of monochrome wares and overglaze enamels along with blue and white wares. Considerable export to the Middle East, with attempts there to imitate Chinese porcelain. **14th-15th centuries:** earthenware with opaque white glaze and colors made in Spain and Italy. **1447:** gift of three Chinese porcelain dishes from the Sultan of Egypt to Charles VII of France. **1517:** first Portuguese ship arrives in the Chinese harbor of Canton. **1520:** Albrecht Dürer on a journey to the Netherlands "ate breakfast with the Portuguese who gave me three porcolana." **1575-1620:** Medici grand-dukes of Florence support Bernardo Buontalenti's manufacture of kaolinic porcelain with blue decoration. **1598:** beginnings of

Japanese porcelain manufacture. **1599/1600:** "The Governor and Company of Merchants of London Trading into the East Indies" chartered in London. **1602:** Dutch East India Company founded. **1604:** first public auction in Amsterdam of porcelain brought from China by a Portuguese ship. **1662-1722:** reign of Emperor K'ang Hsi, favoring porcelain production, mainly at Ching-techen. European merchants permitted to establish offices or "hongs" in the harbor of Canton, to further trade. **17th-18th centuries:** European attempts, in Delft, Holland, and elsewhere, to imitate Chinese porcelain in opaque white glazed faience with blue decoration. **1673:** Louis Poterat in Rouen, France, obtains a patent for his sons from Louis XIV to make soft-paste porcelain containing not kaolin, but ground glass. Production ceases with his son Louis' death in 1696. **1678:** Pierre Chicaneau in St. Cloud invents a soft-paste process, perfected after his death by his son and his widow who receive a patent from the king in 1702. The production continues until 1766. **1709:** first hard porcelain made in Europe by Johann Friedrich Böttger in Dresden, based on experiments with Ehrenfried Walther von Tschirnhausen. **1710:** founding of the Royal Saxon Por-

celain Manufacture by Augustus the Strong and its transfer to Meissen. **1719:** French Compagnie des Deux Indes founded under the Regent Louis Philippe d'Orléans. **1718/1719:** beginnings of the Vienna factory of du Paquier, founded with the help of two workmen from Meissen. **1720:** Francesco Vezzi's factory founded in Venice, also with the aid of a Meissen worker. The arrival of Johann Gregor Herold at Meissen and the beginning of his artistic leadership in production and painting. **1731:** arrival of sculptor Johann Joachim Kändler at Meissen, and the beginning of the Meissen figurines that became prototypes for many other factories. **1735:** founding of factory at Chantilly, France. **1740:** Vincennes, France. **1743:** Capodimonte, Italy. **1745:** Chelsea, England. **1746:** Höchst, Germany. **1748:** Bow, England. **1751:** Worcester, England. **1752:** Frankenthal, Germany. **1753:** Vincennes factory moved to Sèvres. Founding of factory at Nymphenburg, Germany. **1754-1763:** Bustelli master modeller at Nymphenburg. **1758:** Ludwigsburg, Germany. **1759:** Weesp, Holland. **1761:** Berlin. **1763:** Zurich. **1766:** Marieberg, Sweden. **1769:** introduction of hard-paste porcelain to Sèvres. **1774:** Copenhagen. **1825:** Tucker's factory, Philadelphia.

INDEX

Nymphenburg
1757

Nymphenburg
1760